P9-CCU-324

Crafting Fun Stuff
with a
Crowd of Kids

Crafting Fun Stuff with a Crowd of Kids

Carol Scheffler

Sterling Publishing Co., Inc. New York
A Sterling/Chapelle Book

Chapelle, Ltd.

Owner: Jo Packham

Editor: Karmen Potts Quinney

Staff: Areta Bingham, Kass Burchett, Marilyn Goff, Holly Hollingsworth, Susan Jorgensen, Barbara Milburn, Linda Orton, Cindy Stoeckl, Sara Toliver, Desirée Wybrow

Graphic Artist: Kim Taylor

Photo Stylist: Jill Dahlberg

Photography: Kevin Dilley for Hazen Photography

Library of Congress Cataloging-in-Publication Data Available

10 9 8 7 6 5 4 3 2 1

A Sterling/Chapelle Book

First paperback edition published in 2003 by
Sterling Publishing Company, Inc.
387 Park Avenue South, New York, NY 10016
© 2002 by Carol Scheffler
Distributed in Canada by Sterling Publishing
C/o Canadian Manda Group, One Atlantic Avenue, Suite 105
Toronto, Ontario, Canada M6K 3E7
Distributed in Great Britain by Chrysalis Books
64 Brewery Road, London N7 9NT, England
Distributed in Australia by Capricorn Link (Australia) Pty. Ltd.
P.O. Box 704, Windsor, NSW 2756, Australia

Printed in China
All Rights Reserved

ISBN 1-4027-1016-X

A special thank you to Jill Dahlberg, Julie Dixon, and Jill Grover for allowing us to photograph parts of this book in their homes. Their trust and cooperation are greatly appreciated.

Also a special thank you to Ben Dahlberg, Brooke Dahlberg, Bryce Dahlberg, Allison Dixon, Ryan Dixon, Taylor Goodnight, Lauren Mabey, and Mykklyn Stanzione for allowing us to photograph them.

The written instructions, illustrations, photographs, and projects in this volume are intended for the personal use of the reader and may be reproduced for that purpose only. Any other use, especially commercial use, is forbidden under law without the written permission of the copyright holder.

Every effort has been made to ensure that all of the information in this book is accurate. However, due to differing conditions, tools, and individual skills, the publisher cannot be responsible for any injuries, losses, and/or any other damages which may result from the use of the information in this book.

If you have any questions or comments, please contact:

Chapelle, Ltd., Inc.
P.O. Box 9252
Ogden, UT 84409
Phone: (801) 621-2777
FAX: (801) 621-2788
e-mail: Chapelle@chapelleltd.com
website: www.chapelleltd.com

Carol Scheffler is widely recognized in every form of media as one of the foremost authorities on Arts and Crafts.

Carol is a regular arts-and-crafts contributor to morning news and talk shows such as the Today Show and the Rosie O'Donnell Show. She is also a featured guest on leading crafts shows on HGTV, CNN, the Discovery Channel, and PBS.

Carol is also a noted crafts book author. Her latest books include *Family Crafting* and *Rubber Stamping for the First Time*™.

Carol is proud to serve as the Hobby Industry Association's Spokesperson for National Craft Month, observed in March of each year to celebrate the joys of crafting. Carol carries this message across the country, through television and radio appearances and newspaper interviews.

A frequent contributor to many magazines, Carol's designs can be found in *Parents Magazine*, *McCall's*, *Better Homes and Gardens Creative Home*, *Popular Photography*, and *The Rubber Stamper*.

Dedication

This book is dedicated to my own little crowd of kids, Madeline, Eliza, and Susannah, and to the crowds of kids from Murray Avenue School in Larchmont, New York, that I have the pleasure of crafting with. They all bring joy to my life!

Contents

My Nature Journal

Introduction

Dear:

Parents Who Throw Crafting Birthday Parties For Their Children

Camp Counselors

Scout Leaders

Teachers and

Day-care Center Workers

So, you will be leading a group of kids in a craft project and need some inspiration and advice on cute, functional, doable, affordable ideas that the kids will love. And, you are feeling more than a little nervous! If you are like most,

• *Dreaming up craft projects that delight children isn't your forte;*

• *You get a little queasy walking up and down the aisle of a craft store trying to prepare for your youth-oriented crafting adventure; and*

• *You wish you could wake up tomorrow to find that someone has dreamed up the project, purchased the supplies, and figured out the step-by-step instructions so that you could just show up and enjoy the fun.*

Don't worry—I'm here to help! Here is my five-step plan for ensuring a fun, successful, and rewarding experience for you and your children!

Step 1: PAT YOURSELF ON THE BACK!

While taking the time and making the effort to help a group of kids enjoy a little creativity may seem small to you, the truth is there are huge benefits that kids derive from hands-on creative activity.

SKILLS: They will learn skills such as math, language, arts, science, and planning. And unlike so much of the time that kids spend today in a sort of virtual reality—in front of computers, video games, and television—crafting affords a chance to sharpen motor and dexterity skills by allowing them to use their own two hands!

PRIDE: They will be proud of their accomplishments! Kids need the experience of taking raw materials and putting them together in a way that fulfills a vision they have in their heads. It gives them a sense of power and accomplishment unlike anything else. You know how great it is to hear a child say "Come look at what I made!" Additionally, many projects in the book make wonderful gifts to be shared. Kids love sharing their creativity with others and making a personal contribution to a holiday or special event.

FUN: Most important of all, crafting with kids is fun—for everyone involved. It gives you and everyone else a chance to block out the rest of the world and sit down together and enjoy yourselves. As the kids begin working on the project, you will see that they start to relax and socialize almost immediately. Children lead busy lives, often with some measure of stress and anxiety. Crafting together is a great stress buster!

Step 2: PICK A PROJECT.

This book offers you over 40 different project ideas that can be completed identically as shown or changed as desired.

TYPE OF PROJECT: The projects in this book are divided into basic groupings: Nature Crafts, School Supplies, Toys, Room Stuff, Gifts, and Cool Clothes. If you are planning to make several projects with your group of kids over a period of time, vary the projects by type, skill, and materials.

COST: All of the projects were designed to be inexpensive, usually under $1.00 per child, based on a group size of about eight kids. Please be aware that costs vary somewhat from region to region and that the approximated cost assumes that certain materials, like scissors, glue, paper cutters, craft punches, etc., are already owned and do not need to be purchased. In the few instances where a project may cost several dollars per child, I have included ideas for modifying the project in order to reduce the cost.

 DIFFICULTY: I have noted the difficulty level of each project by number of crayons. Very simple projects receive one crayon and can be completed by young children ages 4 and up with some assistance from a grown-up. The most difficult projects in the book are noted with three crayons.

These can be accomplished by children ages 8 and up with some assistance from a grown-up. Children, ages 12 and up, should be able to do all projects on their own. When selecting a project for your particular group of kids, use your best judgement and feel free to modify it. Nearly all of the projects can be completed in one sitting.

Step 3: PURCHASE SUPPLIES.

The projects in this book are created with a variety of materials, all of which have been selected with an eye toward keeping the project cost low while keeping the creativity level high! Nearly everything can be found in a craft store, your recycling bin, your clothes closet, or on a nature walk.

As a first step, I recommend taking inventory of some of the tools/materials you will need to complete the projects. Gather together multiples of the following:

Materials

Craft glue
Craft punches
Craft scissors
Glue sticks
Paintbrushes
Pencils
Pens
Rulers

When crafting with a group of kids, the rule of thumb I use is:

1 pair of craft scissors and 1 glue stick for every two kids

1 bottle of glue or paint, craft punch, and ruler for every three to four kids

1 handful of markers for every five to six kids

IDEAS:

Utilize household items to minimize costs. For example:

A piece of foil or a disposable plate makes a great paint pallet.

Use empty yogurt cups to hold paint.

Keep papers, pom-poms, and other small items separate on clean disposable food trays.

Cover tables and floors with plastic tablecloths.

Paper towels and a jug of water help to clean up spills.

ADULT SUPERVISION

Adult supervision is required when using an iron, craft knife, serrated knife, and power drill.

Step 4: MAKE A SAMPLE PROJECT.

Making a sample project accomplishes three things:

1 Kids love to see a sample of the project they will be making. It serves as a guidepost in helping them visualize the steps to follow and it provides design inspiration. However, make certain the kids understand that they are the designer of their own project and that it does not have to look like yours.

2 By making a sample, you will become more familiar with the steps and challenges of the particular project and will better be able to assist the children and answer their questions.

3 Making a sample gives you the chance to modify the project, if you so desire.

Step 5: PRESENT THE PROJECT.

Welcome the kids to the craft table. Expect some jitters and a little bit of apprehension.

Have the materials organized and spread evenly across the table.

Wait to show the completed project until all the kids are assembled and attentive.

Once you have shown the completed project to the children, introduce them to the materials on the table, explaining how to use them safely. Remind the children to share the materials. Encourage them to use their creativity to make the project their own.

Be on hand to answer questions and offer encouragement.

Arrange for an assistant for groups larger than eight kids, particularly if the kids are very young.

Following these five steps will make the entire process of crafting with a group of children easy, fun, and fulfilling. Have a terrific time!

Best,

Carol Scheffler

Carol Scheffler

GENERAL INSTRUCTIONS

Dry-brushing

1 Using paintbrush, dip paintbrush into paint, then rub paintbrush back and forth on plate to distribute paint into paintbrush.

2 Rub paintbrush on paper towel to remove excess paint. When paint begins to have a powder-like look, apply paint to project.

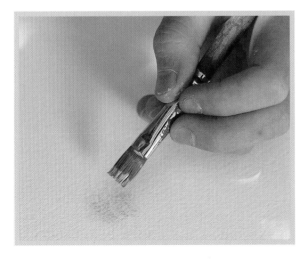

Baste Stitch

A line of straight stitches with an unstitched area between each stitch.

1 Come up at A and down at B.

My
Nature
Journal

Rememb
rake t
leav

Da

Nature Crafts

Sam called

Sam called again

RAIN STICK

Instructions

1. Hammer brads into tube 1" apart over entire tube. Make certain to stagger placement of brads.

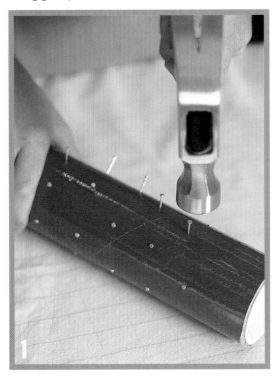

2. Glue one cap onto end of tube. Pour rice into tube. Glue remaining cap onto other end of tube.

Materials

Brads: ¾" (1 box)
Card stock: assorted colors
Cardboard mailing tube
Craft glue
Craft scissors
Hammer
Mailing paper: brown
Uncooked rice (1 cup)
Water
Yarn

3. Mix craft glue and water. Dip brown paper into mixture and completely cover tube for rain stick.

4. Embellish rain stick with card stock and yarn as desired.

Materials

Acrylic paints: black; orange; turquoise; yellow

Burlap: 15"-square

Coordinating thread

Paintbrushes

Pony beads: red (4)

Sewing needle

Sticks

Stones: smooth (12)

Twine

Yarn

4 Fold length of burlap in half. See Baste Stitch on page 13. Using needle and thread, baste-stitch up one end and side of burlap with fold on opposite side. Attach beads at top, stitched corner. Fray all around by pulling horizontal threads from edges.

5 Place stones and sticks inside sack.

6 Braid yarn and twine together for tie cord. Tie sack closed with cord.

Instructions

1 Paint six stones with turquoise paint. Paint remaining stones with yellow paint. Let dry.

2 Paint an "X" on turquoise stones with yellow paint then black paint. Paint an "O" on yellow stones with black paint. Let dry.

3 Paint sticks as desired.

TREASURE MOBILE

Instructions

1 Cross and tie sticks together with twine for mobile.

2 Tie desired length of twine from center top of mobile for hanger.

3 Tie nature elements onto mobile with twine. Make certain that the weight of elements is balanced so that sticks will hang level. *Note: Two or more elements can be tied on the same piece of twine.*

A nature walk can provide everything needed to make this fascinating mobile. As you collect your nature elements, be certain not to gather or disturb anything that might be home to a living creature. Shells, cocoons, and pods should be empty.

Materials

Nature elements: bark; bones; feathers; grasses; leaves; pods; seashells

Sticks (2)

Twine

My Nature Journal

Instructions

1. Punch two holes in bottom of each paper bag. See photograph on facing page. Stack bags on top of each other. Make certain that holes are aligned.

2. Push loop of one rubber band through one set of holes in stack from back to front. Push loop on other end of same rubber band through remaining hole from back to front.

3. Thread stick through rubber band loops.

4. Cut out leaves, acorns, and circles for bugs from colored paper. Glue onto top bag for journal cover.

5. Tie raffia around rubber band and stick.

6. Draw leaves and bugs on cover as desired.

7. Write title of journal on cover as desired.

IDEA:

Use die-cuts to make this project really easy. Die-cuts are paper shapes that are already cut out. You can find them in craft stores.

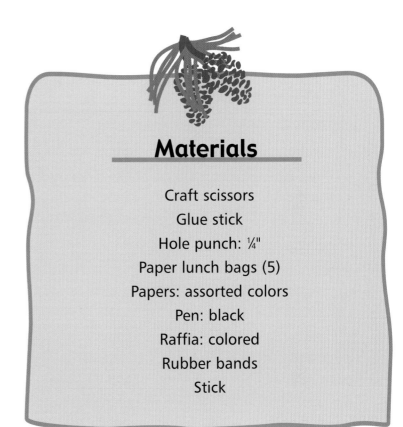

Materials

Craft scissors
Glue stick
Hole punch: ¼"
Paper lunch bags (5)
Papers: assorted colors
Pen: black
Raffia: colored
Rubber bands
Stick

Taking a nature walk can be memorable at any time of the year. There are always things to discover. Create this journal made from paper bags so that you have a place to store all the little treasures you might find. Label each page of the journal with the bag's contents and describe where and when you found it.

WOVEN WALL HANGING

Materials

Burlap: 7" x 14"

Craft glue

Craft scissors

Large-eyed needle

Leather shoelace

Nature elements: bark; bones; feathers;
grasses; leaves; pods

Ruler

Sewing needle

Small pinecones

Stick: 12"

Twine

Instructions

1 Fray sides of burlap ½" by pulling long vertical threads from edges. Set pulled threads aside.

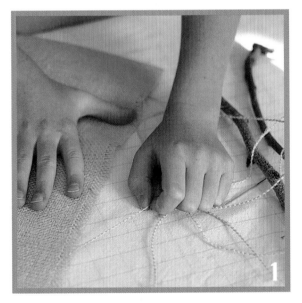

2 Fold top of burlap over stick. See Baste Stitch on page 13. Using needle and one long thread pulled from sides, baste-stitch stick inside of fold.

3 Randomly pull out burlap threads horizontally in 1" sections.

4 Weave nature elements in and out of vertical threads.

5 Tie beads, buttons, and pinecones to bottom edge.

6 Measure length of shoelace, then double measurement.

7 Cut twine to doubled measurement.

8 Fold twine in half. Place one end of shoelace at fold of twine. Braid shoelace and twine together for hanger.

9 Tie hanger to ends of stick.

School
Supplies

Science
Project
due on
Monday.

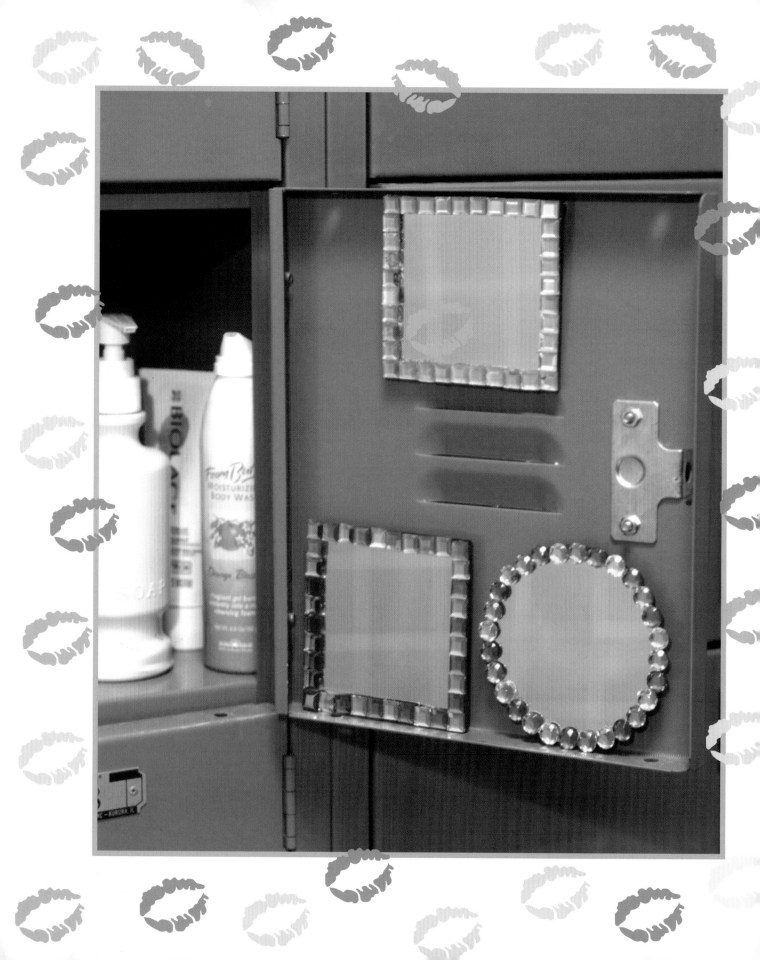

Jeweled Locker Mirrors

Instructions

1 Glue three magnets onto back of each square mirror. Glue two magnets onto back of round mirror.

2 Arrange and glue square rhinestones around edges of square mirrors, alternating colors as desired.

3 Arrange and glue round rhinestones around edges of round mirror, alternating colors as desired. Let dry.

Your locker is your little oasis at school. Give it some dazzling personality with these trendy jeweled mirrors.

Materials

Extra-strength magnets (8)

Glass glue

Round mirror: 4"-diameter

Round rhinestones: citrine, 10mm (9); green, 10mm (9); turquoise, 10mm (9)

Square mirrors: 4" (2)

Square rhinestones: citrine, 10mm (18); pink, 10mm (36); turquoise, 10mm (18)

ASIAN PENCIL BOX

Instructions

1 Paint box with white paint. Let dry.

2 Cut out small sections from newspaper.

3 Using sponge brush, spread decoupage medium onto box. Layer small sections of newspaper onto outside of box. Spread decoupage medium over newspaper sections. Continue until box is covered. Let dry.

Materials

Acrylic paint: white
Card stock: red
Chinese newspaper
Craft glue
Craft scissors
Decoupage medium
Paintbrush
Sponge brush
Thread: gold
Wooden box

4 Trim any edges that extend beyond box.

5 Spread a layer of decoupage medium over entire box. Let dry.

6 Cut 3" strip from card stock. Accordion-fold strip into a fan. Fold strip in half to double width of fun. Glue interior edges of fan together.

7 Tie gold thread around bottom of fan. See photograph on facing page. Dot craft glue on fan to hold thread in place.

8 Glue fan onto box front.

JUNGLE NOTEBOOKS

Take a walk on the wild side with these totally trendy notebooks that take minutes to make.

Materials

Fabric glue

Fabric marker

Fabric scissors

Faux-fur fabric: (½ yd)

Notebook

Instructions

1 Lay fabric wrong side up on work surface. Trace notebook cover onto back side of fabric.

2 Cut out fabric cover.

3 Glue fabric cover onto front of notebook.

IDEAS:

Weave beaded wire onto spirals of notebook.

Embellish notebook covers with feathers, craft jewels, or buttons.

Perky Pens

Homework will be a pleasure when using these pens. Or give them as a gift with a handmade diary or journal. The pens featured below were created with colored string and various beads.

Instructions

1 Beginning at writing end of pen, wrap tape around pen. Make certain to cover pen completely.

2 Glue decorative element to end of pen.

Note: Pens can be wrapped first with chenille stem, then wrapped with tape to give more dimension.

Materials

Ballpoint pens

Chenille stems (optional)

Decorative element such as: balls; beads; butterflies; fabric trims; rhinestones

Floral tape: lt. green

Hot-glue gun/glue sticks

IDEA:

Try creating pens with colored floss and beads. Wrap pens with floss, beginning at writing end. Leave extra floss at the end, then thread beads onto string. Knot to secure.

CREATURE FOOTPRINTS

Materials

Acrylic paints: brown; orange; turquoise; yellow

Craft glue

Craft knife

Gum eraser

Mailing paper: brown

Notebook

Paper towels

Pen

Pencil

Plastic plates

Sponge brush

Instructions

1 Lay mailing paper wrong side up on work surface. Place open notebook face down onto mailing paper. Trace around entire notebook.

2 Cut out mailing paper cover.

3 Glue mailing paper cover onto notebook front, back, and binding.

4 Draw animal footprints or bird footprints as desired onto eraser.

5 Using craft knife, cut away unwanted area from design for stamp.

6 Place paper towel inside of notebook.

7 Pour a quarter-sized amount of brown paint onto a paper plate.

8 Using sponge brush, daub paint onto stamp, covering entire area.

9 Press stamp down firmly on notebook, then lift stamp straight up so that print does not smear. Repeat as desired.

10 Repeat Steps 5–9 with orange, turquoise, and yellow paint. *Note: Rinse stamps and brush between paint colors.* Let dry.

Dee Park
at
5:30

Toys

Roller blades
Water bottle
HAT
Jacket

Little Green Alien

Help! . . . we're being invaded by the silliest aliens ever seen. Perch these little green guys any place you want to make someone smile. Vary the instructions given here to create an original little green guy who's out-of-this-world.

Instructions

1 Paint egg with green paint for alien. Let dry.

2 Using craft scissors, cut metallic stems in half. Insert three half stems into wide end of alien for legs. See photograph on facing page.

3 Add drop of glue into each hole to secure legs. Let dry.

4 Cut two 1¼" lengths from bright green stem. Insert lengths into side of alien for arms.

5 Add drop of glue into each hole to secure arms. Let dry.

6 Cut feet and hands from the same shade of felt. Bend leg ends as necessary and glue feet onto legs. Glue hands onto arms. Let dry.

Materials

Acrylic paint: dk. green

Chenille stems: bright green, 12"; metallic green, 12" (2)

Craft scissors

Felt (scraps): assorted greens

Paintbrush

Pom-poms: bright green, ¼"-diameter (9); orange, ¼"-diameter

Styrofoam™ egg: 3"

Tacky craft glue

Wiggly eye: glow in the dark

Wooden skewers

Yarn: assorted greens

7 Glue three green pom-poms onto each foot for toes.

8 Glue eye onto alien. Glue orange pom-pom onto alien for nose.

9 Cut cheeks, hair, and mouth from remaining felt scraps. Glue onto alien as desired.

10 Using skewer, make hole in back of alien. Knot yarn. Dip knot into craft glue. Insert knot into hole for tail. Let dry.

Seashell Tic-tac-toe

Instructions 🖍🖍

1 Place eight craft sticks vertically side by side, forming 5⅞" square. Glue three craft sticks horizontally across the square as shown in Diagram A. *Note: This will be the back side.* Let dry.

Diagram A

2 Paint one side of square with dk. blue paint. Let dry. Repeat for remaining side.

3 Place two pieces of scallop tape vertically on front of square. Place two pieces of scallop tape horizontally across square, creating nine equal sections. Paint front of square with lt. blue paint. Peel off tape, revealing waves of dk. blue paint.

Materials

Acrylic paints: dk. blue; lt. blue; lt. mauve; yellow

Craft glue

Fine-tipped permanent marker: brown

Jumbo craft sticks (11)

Paintbrushes

Scallop-edged tape: ½"-wide

Wooden stars: 1⅝" (5)

Wooden teardrops: 2" (5)

4 Paint one side of teardrops with lt. mauve paint for seashells. Paint stars with yellow paint for starfish. Let dry. Repeat for remaining sides.

5 Draw a wiggly line around both sides of dk. blue waves. See photograph on facing page.

6 Draw dots on lt. blue section of square. Draw details as desired on seashells and starfish.

Sailboat

Instructions

1 Photocopy Sailboat Pattern on page 46 and Sail Pattern on page 47 at photocopy center. Cut out patterns.

2 Using pencil, trace Sailboat Pattern onto 1" x 3½" x 6" Styrofoam™ sheet. Trace Sail Pattern onto fabric.

3 Using knife, cut out sailboat. Using craft scissors, cut out sail. Using fingertips, smooth Styrofoam™.

4 Cut 2" x 3" piece from remaining Styrofoam™ sheet for sailboat cab.

5 Paint sailboat with paint. Paint 1¼" dowel with same paint color for rudder. Paint sailboat cab with remaining paint. Let dry.

6 Fold fabric side and bottom over towards center. Pin fold. See Baste Stitch on page 13. Baste-stitch along edge of folded fabric for channels for mast and boom. Sew across top end of mast channel but not bottom end or on either end of boom channel.

7 Sew 6" length of thread to outer tip of sail. Set aside.

8 Using waterproof pens, decorate sail as desired.

Continued on page 46.

Materials

Acrylic paints: contrasting colors (2)

Cotton fabric: 7½" x 8½"

Craft scissors

Low-temperature glue gun/glue sticks

Photocopier

Serrated steak knife

Sewing needle

Stiff paintbrushes

Straight pins

Styrofoam™ sheets: 1" x 3" x 6"; 1" x 3½" x 6"

Thread: white

Waterproof pens: assorted colors

Wooden dowel ³⁄₁₆"-diameter: 1¼"; 5"; 9"

Continued from page 45.

9 Push 9" dowel down into front of sailboat for mast. Glue to secure.

10 Push rudder down into back of sailboat. Push 5" dowel into boom channel.

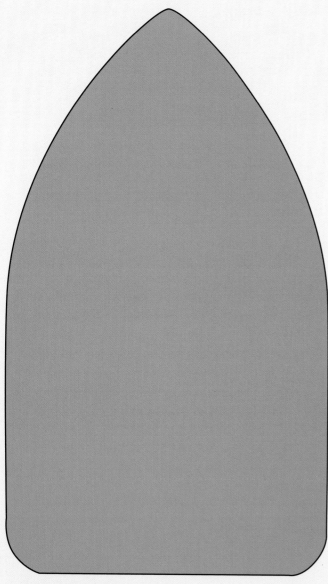

Sailboat Pattern

11 Push side channel over mast until mast hits top seam.

12 Tie thread at tip of sail around rudder to keep sail in place while sailing.

IDEAS:

Freedom's Sail

Delaney's Voyage

Sail Pattern

BRIGHT BOWLING

Here's a recipe for double fun. Craft these cute bowling pins, then challenge your friends to a tournament.

Instructions

Note: Make certain that bottles and lids are clean and dry.

1 Paint outside of bottles with lime green paint. Let dry.

2 Drop twelve marbles into each container. Replace lids.

3 Center square of fabric over top of container and secure on neck with rubber band.

4 Glue trim as desired.

5 Play the game by knocking down the pins with a rubber ball. Whoever, knocks down the most pins, wins.

Materials

Acrylic paint: lime green
Craft glue
Fabric: 8"-square
Large rubber ball
Marbles (72)
Paintbrushes
Rubber bands (6)
Soda bottles: 2-liter (6)
Trims

Ice Cream Cone Game

When is ice cream too good to eat? When it is a fun ball & toss game made from Styrofoam™ and paint.

Instructions

1. Using teaspoon, hollow out wide end of cone, removing small amounts of foam at a time. *Note: The hole should hold 3" Styrofoam™ ball comfortably.* Using back side of teaspoon, smooth out hole.

2. Insert skewer into narrow end of Styrofoam™ cone. Holding skewer, paint cone with tan paint. Let dry. Remove skewer.

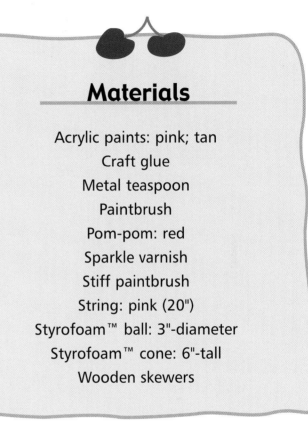

Materials

Acrylic paints: pink; tan

Craft glue

Metal teaspoon

Paintbrush

Pom-pom: red

Sparkle varnish

Stiff paintbrush

String: pink (20")

Styrofoam™ ball: 3"-diameter

Styrofoam™ cone: 6"-tall

Wooden skewers

3. Insert skewer into side of Styrofoam™ ball. Holding skewer, paint ball with pink paint for ice cream.

4. Apply sparkle varnish to cone, following manufacturer's instructions. Let dry.

5. Tie knots in both ends of string. Place a drop of glue into skewer hole in cone and ice cream hole. Insert a knot. Let dry.

6. Glue pom-pom onto top of ice cream. Let dry.

Periscope Adventures

Materials

Craft glue
Craft knife
Fabric (scraps)
Mailing paper: brown
Masking tape
Narrow box or mailing tube
Plastic camping mirrors (2)
Twine

Instructions

1 Using craft knife, cut two slits at 45° angles on opposite sides and at each end of box for mirrors as shown in Diagram A.

Diagram A

2 Cut out 2" x 4" rectangle from box front top and back bottom for view opening as shown in Diagram B.

Diagram B

3 Make certain ends of box are closed. *Note: If using a mailing tube, make certain that the lid fits tightly on the tube.* Mix craft glue and water. Dip brown paper into mixture and completely cover box. Do not cover slits. Let dry.

4 Slide mirrors into slits and secure with tape. See photograph on facing page.

5 Embellish periscope with fabric scraps.

IDEA:
This periscope was made from a mailing tube.

Mini Sand Castle

Instructions

1 Using knife, cut two 6" x 8" pieces, two 6"-square pieces, and four 1" x 2" pieces from Styrofoam™ sheet for walls.

2 Photocopy Door Pattern below.

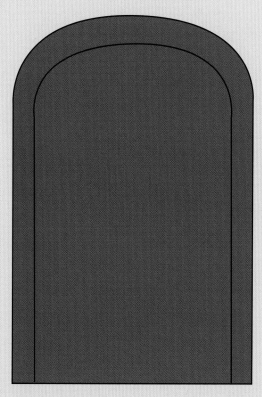

Door Pattern

3 Using craft scissors, cut out pattern. Using pencil, trace pattern onto one 6" x 8" piece of Styrofoam™. Set pattern aside. Using knife, cut out door.

Materials

Cardboard (scrap)
Chenille stem: brown (12")
Craft glue
Craft picks: 3½" (25)
Craft scissors
Darning needle
Felt: assorted colors
Masking tape
Pencil
Photocopier
Rocks
Ruler
Sandbox sand
Serrated steak knife
Sphagnum moss
Stiff paintbrush: 1"
String: brown (26")
Styrofoam™ cones: 2" x 3" (4)
Styrofoam™ sheet: 1" x 12" x 18"
Superthick brown foamie
Wooden skewer

4 Glue walls together, placing wall with door and remaining 6" x 8" piece of Styrofoam™ opposite of each other for castle front and back. Let dry.

5 Glue 1"-square strips into each of the four interior corners. Let dry.

6 Glue inverted cones onto top of each corner. Let dry.

7 Spread craft glue evenly over interior surface of castle. Do not let dry.

8 Quickly sprinkle sand onto wet, glued surfaces. Using fingertips, gently press sand into glue. Shake off excess sand.

9 Continue gluing and sanding process until entire castle is covered. *Note: Leave one tower unsanded until the very end to give yourself something to hold onto while working.*

10 Using fingertips, gently press rocks along top edge while glue is still wet. Add a drop of glue if necessary to set rocks in place. Let dry.

11 Trace pattern onto foamie for bridge. Using craft scissors, cut out bridge.

12 Using darning needle, pierce two holes through top of bridge.

13 Using craft scissors, cut and discard ¼" from each end of four craft picks. Glue two craft picks side by side toward top of bridge for planks as shown in Diagram A. Glue two remaining craft picks side by side toward bottom of bridge. Let dry.

Diagram A

14 Glue one craft pick onto back bottom edge of bridge. Let dry.

15 Loop a 4" piece of masking tape and place on cardboard. Press a line of 10–12 craft picks ⅛" apart onto tape for portcullis.

16 Center and glue one craft pick across line of craft picks as shown in Diagram B. Glue one craft pick ¼" down from one end. Glue another craft pick ½" up from opposite end. Let dry. Remove tape.

Diagram B

17 Cut two 4" lengths from string. Knot one end of each length to each top corner of portcullis. Knot remaining ends together.

18 Using skewer, pierce a hole through wall ¼" up from top right side of door opening. Repeat on left side of door opening.

19 Cut two 10" lengths from string. Knot one end of each length. Thread unknotted end of string through each hole in bridge and each hole in wall, going from front to back. Knot remaining ends together. Pull string to close bridge. Loosen string to open.

20 Cut chenille stem into 3" sections. Bend two chenille stems into u-shaped loops.

21 Insert over each end of craft pick on back bottom edge of bridge. See photograph below. Press loops into wall ¼" up from bottom of door for bridge hinges. Make certain loops are secure in wall but loose enough so that the bridge can easily fold up and down. Add a drop of glue in each hole to secure.

22 Cut 1" length from remaining section of chenille stem. Press 1" length into inside wall above door and bend stem up for portcullis hook.

23 Glue rocks around bottom edge of castle.

24 Glue bits of moss in between rocks and onto castle.

25 Using craft scissors, cut four ¾" x 2" rectangles from felt.

26 Fold one felt piece in half lengthwise. Cut end of ribbon diagonally from corner point on one end for flag. Repeat for remaining felt pieces.

27 Glue flags onto craft pick. Center and glue craft pick onto castle corners.

28 Cut eleven triangles as desired from felt. Cut 6" length from string.

29 Glue triangles onto string. Glue end of string onto top front of castle. See photograph below.

Halloween Puppets & Theater

Instructions

(for Halloween Puppets)

1. Snap off and set aside double end section from each end of skill sticks. Discard center sections. *Note: This will give you four sections: one for Frankenstein's bolts, one for vampire's ears, one for witch's hat brim, and one for scarecrow's hat brim.*

2. Lightly sand snapped edges if necessary.

Materials

Acrylic paints: lt. brown; olive green; lavender; pumpkin; purple; red; silver; turquoise; white; lt. yellow

Craft glue

Fine-grit sandpaper

Fine-tipped permanent marker with bullet: black

Jumbo craft sticks (5)

Paintbrushes

Paper towels

Skill sticks (2)

Toothpick

Wiggly eyes: round (10)

Wooden circles: ⅜"-diameter (5)

IDEA:

Create a puppet theater using nursery tale rhymes like *Three Little Pigs* and *Little Red Riding Hood*, or create your own cast of characters.

Instructions
(for Ghost)

1 Paint one side of one craft stick and one circle for nose with white paint. Let dry. Repeat for remaining sides.

2 Using fine-tipped end of marker, draw head shape onto craft stick as desired. See photograph on right.

3 See Dry-brushing on page 13. Dry-brush cheeks with pumpkin paint.

4 Using toothpick, dot cheeks with white paint.

5 Using bullet end of marker, draw wavy vertical stripes on body.

6 Glue eyes and nose onto face. Let dry.

Instructions
(for Frankenstein)

1 Paint one side of one craft stick and one circle for nose with olive green paint. Paint one skill stick section for neck bolt with silver paint. Let dry. Repeat for remaining sides.

2 Using fine-tipped end of marker, draw head shape onto craft stick as desired. See photograph on right.

3 Dry-brush cheeks with pumpkin paint.

4 Using toothpick, dot cheeks with white paint.

5 Draw mouth, hair, scars, and bottom of head. Outline edges of neck bolts.

6 Using bullet end of marker, draw wavy vertical stripes on body.

7 Glue eyes and nose onto face. Center and glue neck bolts onto back of neck. Let dry.

Instructions
(for Scarecrow)

1 Paint one side of one craft stick, except for one end, with lt. yellow paint. See photograph on right. Let dry. Repeat for remaining sides.

2 Paint remaining end for hat and one skill stick section for hat brim with lt. brown paint. Paint one circle for nose with red paint. Repeat for remaining sides.

3 Using fine-tipped end of marker, draw bottom of head.

4 Dry-brush cheeks with pumpkin paint.

5 Using toothpick, dot cheeks with white paint.

6 Using bullet end of marker, draw wavy vertical stripes on body. Using fine-tipped end, draw details on hat and brim.

7 Draw mouth and straw coming down from hat.

8 Glue hat brim onto bottom of hat. Glue eyes and nose onto face.

Instructions
(for Vampire)

1 Paint one side of one craft stick, one circle for nose, and one skill stick section for ears with turquoise paint. Let dry. Repeat for re-maining sides.

2 Using fine-tipped end of marker, draw head shape on craft stick. Draw details on ears. See photo-graph on right.

3 Dry-brush cheeks with pumpkin paint.

4 Using toothpick, dot cheeks with white paint.

5 Draw mouth, teeth, hair, and bottom of head. Paint teeth with white paint.

6 Using bullet end of marker, draw wavy vertical stripes on body.

7 Glue eyes and nose onto face. Center and glue ears onto back of head. Let dry.

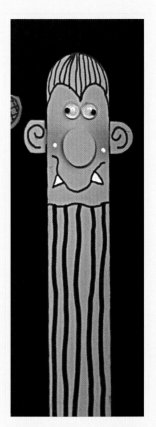

After creating the Halloween Puppets, design a theater to show them off. Use the Theater by standing the shoe box with opening in front for stage. Place theater along the back edge of a surface.

ADMIT ONE

Materials

Coordinating thread
Cord
Craft knife
Craft scissors
Decorative-edged scissors: pinking
Fabric
Masking tape
Newspaper
Pencil
Ruler
Safety pin
Sewing needle
Shoe box
Spray paint: black
Tacky glue

Instructions
(for Theater)

1 Cover work surface with newspaper. Spray-paint shoe box, following manufacturer's instructions. Let dry.

2 Determine side for bottom. Measure and mark 1" in from each side of bottom. Measure ½" from back edge of box. Draw 1"-wide opening as shown in Diagram A. Using craft knife and ruler, cut out opening for theater bottom. *Note: The opening is where the puppets will be inserted for the puppet show.*

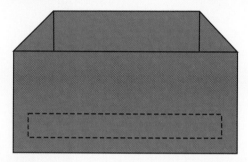

Diagram A

3 Using decorative-edged scissors, cut rectangle 1" longer and ¾" wider than theater front from fabric.

4 Using decorative-edged scissors, cut rectangle in half widthwise. Fold top edge of one curtain ¾" over to wrong side of fabric. See Baste Stitch on page 13. Using sewing needle and coordinating thread, stitch ½" in from folded edge for curtain casing. Repeat for other curtain.

5 Using craft scissors, cut cord 6" longer than theater front. Cover both ends of cord with masking tape, then twist into points. Attach safety pin to one end of cord but not on masking tape. Using safety pin, feed end of cord through curtain casings. Remove safety pin.

6 Using craft knife and a twisting motion, create a small hole in each top front side of theater for cord to go through.

7 Insert taped ends of cord through holes, going from inside to the outside. Knot one cord end on outside of theater. Pull cord taut and knot on opposite side of theater. Dot glue onto each knot to secure in place. Using craft scissors, trim ends.

8 Adjust curtains as necessary.

Treat Bag

Instructions

1 Fold top of pillowcase down 4" and iron in place. Fold down 1" from new top. Pin along entire edge.

2 Sew along pinned edge for channel. Remove pins.

3 Cut one small opening in channel on each side of bag. Attach safety pin to one edge of ribbon. Using safety pin, feed ribbon through channel. Remove safety pin. Sew ends of ribbon together.

4 Using pencil, draw bats, ghosts, stars, and pumpkins onto separate compressed sponges. Cut out shapes. Place in water to expand. Wring out sponge.

5 Lay pillowcase out flat on work surface. Place cardboard inside pillowcase between front and back. *Note: This will keep paint from going through to other side.*

Materials

Cardboard (large scrap)

Compressed sponges

Craft scissors

Fabric glue

Fabric marker: black

Fabric paints: black; orange; purple; yellow

Iron/ironing board

Pillowcase

Plastic plates

Pencil

Ruler

Sewing machine

Straight pins

Sturdy ribbon: 1"-wide (2 yds)

Water

Wiggly eyes

6 Pour a quarter-sized amount of each paint color onto separate plastic plates. Daub sponge into paint and press sponge onto pillowcase front. Walk your fingers along back of sponge and lift sponge straight off.

7 Continue to sponge-paint pillowcase front as desired. Let dry.

8 Using marker, outline images.

9 Glue eyes onto pillowcase. Let dry and remove cardboard from inside of bag.

Clean your room
before your
friends come
over.
                Mom

Slumber Party
Next Friday

Room Stuff

Call Jan

kitty pillow

It's fun to snuggle up with a pet . . . and here's one that is always ready to snuggle back. Sew this kitty pillow from felt and buttons in no time flat.

Instructions

1. Enlarge Kitty Pattern on page 70. *Note: This is done by placing pattern directly in photocopier and enlarging by required percentage.* Cut out pattern.

2. Using pencil, trace pattern onto fabric two times.

3. Cut out pieces.

4. Sew black buttons onto one piece of fabric with white floss for eyes. Sew pink button below eyes with white floss for nose.

5. See Baste Stitch on page 13. Thread needle and knot ends. Baste-stitch whiskers, beginning at nose. See photograph on facing page.

6. Stitch pieces together with white floss, leaving 3" opening at bottom of kitty.

7. Stuff kitty full, but do not overstuff.

8. Stitch opening closed.

Materials

Buttons: black (2); pink
Craft scissors
Embroidery floss: black; white
Embroidery needle
Felt: pink (½ yd)
Pencil
Photocopier
Polyester filling

IDEAS:

You can cut the felt into any shape you like. Stars, hearts, clubs, diamonds, and aces would all make great pillows. Try cutting out letters and create pillows, using your initials or any other word.

Turn the kitty pillow into a purse by leaving the top of the head open and not stuffing it. Add a shoulder strap, using ribbon.

Kitty Pattern   Enlarge 126%

Egghead People

Egghead People

Materials

Acrylic paints: bright colors

Craft scissors

Extra-tacky craft glue

Fast-sprouting rye grass seed

Felt: assorted colors

Metal teaspoon

Rich potting soil

Serrated steak knife

Styrofoam™ balls: 1"; 1½"; 3"

Styrofoam™ egg: 4"

Wiggly eyes: 1"

Instructions

1 Using knife, slice off a small section from wide end of egg.

2 Using teaspoon, scoop small amounts of foam from wide end of egg until hole is 1¼"–1½" deep. Using back side of spoon, smooth hole.

3 Using knife, slice off a small section from narrow end of egg for base.

4 Slice 3" ball in half. Slice off a small section from rounded side of one half-ball as shown in Diagram A.

Diagram A

Create these wacky egghead people with Styrofoam™, glue, and paint. They are simply silly with their grass hair. Place in a sunny location in your room. Remember to water it.

5 Twist narrow end of egg and rounded side of half-ball together until they fit tightly. Glue egg and half-ball together for egghead.

6 Cut 1½" ball in half. Slice off a small section from one side of each half-ball for ears. See photographs at right. Glue each half-ball onto egghead with flat side forward. Let dry.

7 Glue 1" ball onto center front of egg for nose. Let dry.

8 Paint egghead with paints as desired.

9 Glue eyes onto egghead.

10 Using craft scissors, cut out facial features and decorations from felt as desired.

11 Glue felt features and decorations onto egghead.

12 Fill top of egghead with rich potting soil. Sprinkle fast-sprouting rye grass seed onto dirt.

13 Using fingertips, press seeds into dirt.

14 Gently water, then wait until water has been absorbed completely before adding more water. Keep dirt damp but not soaked until grass sprouts.

15 Place in sunlight for good growth. Using craft scissors, trim as desired.

CLAY POT BUG

Instructions

1 Paint pot with olive green paint. Paint bead with fuchsia paint.

2 Glue eyes onto pot. See photograph on facing page.

3 Draw mouth on pot rim.

4 Using end of paintbrush handles, dot four dots on each side of face with fuchsia paint.

5 Thread chenille stems through bead, with ends even on both sides. Thread stem ends through pot hole, from outside to inside. Dot glue around pot hole and secure bead and stems in place.

6 Bend chenille stems upward at bottom of pot for legs. Position three legs at each side of pot. Bend legs downward, then up again at ends.

Materials

Acrylic paints: fuchsia; olive green
Chenille stems: metallic black, 12" (3)
Craft glue
Medium-tipped permanent marker: black
Paintbrushes
Terra-cotta pot: 2½"-diameter
Wiggly eyes: oval, 15mm (2)
Wooden bead: ⅜"-diameter

FUNKY PILLOWCASE

Instructions

1. Fold fleece in half widthwise. *Note: Selvage edges will be pillowcase opening and fold will be bottom of pillowcase.*

2. See Baste Stitch on page 13. Thread needle and knot ends. Baste-stitch side seams, taking ¾" seams.

3. Measure and cut boa to fit around pillowcase opening.

4. Baste-stitch boa to top of pillowcase opening.

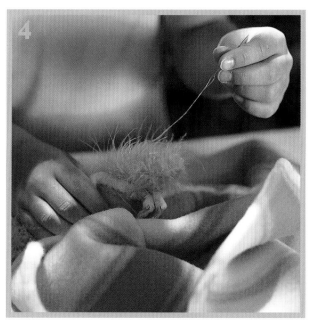

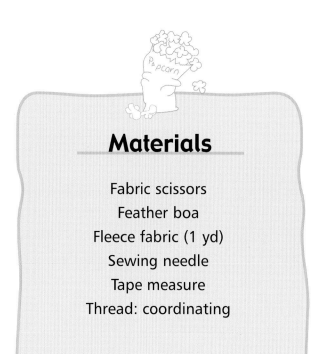

Materials

Fabric scissors
Feather boa
Fleece fabric (1 yd)
Sewing needle
Tape measure
Thread: coordinating

Arrive in style with a totally funky pillowcase that can be used to haul pj's, stuffed animals, and other necessities.

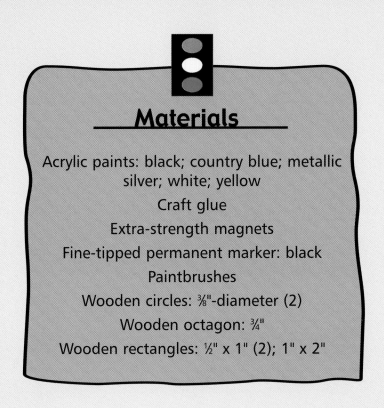

Materials

Acrylic paints: black; country blue; metallic silver; white; yellow

Craft glue

Extra-strength magnets

Fine-tipped permanent marker: black

Paintbrushes

Wooden circles: ⅜"-diameter (2)

Wooden octagon: ¾"

Wooden rectangles: ½" x 1" (2); 1" x 2"

Instructions
(for Personalized Truck Magnet)

1 Paint one side of large rectangle with white paint. Paint one small rectangle with yellow paint. Paint remaining rectangle and octagon with country blue paint. Paint circles with black paint. Let dry. Repeat for remaining sides.

2 Using end of paintbrush handle, dot center of each circle with metallic silver paint for wheels.

3 Draw vertical stripes on white rectangle. Draw stitch marks around edges of yellow rectangle. Write desired name on yellow rectangle. See photograph on right.

4 Draw window on top right corner of octagon as shown in Diagram A. Paint window with black paint.

Diagram A

5 Center and glue yellow rectangle onto front of white rectangle.

6 Glue white rectangle onto left edge of country blue rectangle for truck back.

7 Glue bottom portion of octagon onto back of blue rectangle for truck front.

8 Glue one wheel onto truck front and one onto truck back.

9 Glue magnets onto back of truck.

Materials

Acrylic paints: black; lavender; metallic silver

Craft glue

Craft pick

Extra-strength magnets

Mini craft stick

Paintbrushes

Wooden circles: ⅜"-diameter (5)

Wooden rectangle: ½" x 1"

Instructions
(for Tanker Truck Magnet)

1 Paint one side of rectangle with lavender paint. Paint craft stick and craft pick with metallic silver paint. Paint circles with black paint. Let dry. Repeat for remaining sides.

2 Using end of paintbrush handle, dot center of each circle with metallic silver paint for wheels.

3 Draw window in top corner of rectangle. Paint window with black paint.

4 Glue bottom corner of rectangle onto one end of craft pick for truck front. See photograph below. Glue craft stick horizontally onto remaining end of craft pick for truck back.

5 Glue one wheel onto truck front. Glue four wheels onto truck back. Let dry.

6 Glue magnets onto back of truck.

Instructions
(for Bus Magnet)

1 Cut ends from craft pick so that center measures 2".

2 Draw lines on rectangle for bus and bus windows. See photograph below. Paint bus windows with white paint. Paint bus with royal blue paint. Paint one side of craft pick with red paint. Paint circles with black paint. Let dry. Repeat for remaining sides.

3 Using end of paintbrush handle, dot center of each circle with metallic silver paint for wheels. Let dry.

4 Draw window details and the word "BUS" as desired. Draw stitch marks through center of craft pick.

5 Glue one wheel onto bus front. Glue remaining wheel onto bus back. Let dry.

Materials

Acrylic paints: black; royal blue; red; metallic silver; white

Craft glue

Craft pick

Craft scissors

Extra-strength magnet

Fine-tipped permanent marker: black

Paintbrushes

Ruler

Scissors

Wooden circles: ⅜"-diameter (2)

Wooden rectangle: 1" x 2"

6 Glue red pick above wheels and below the word "BUS."

7 Glue magnet onto back of bus.

Puzzle Piece Frame

A puzzle doesn't have to be thrown away just because a few pieces are missing. Use the remaining pieces to decorate a picture frame. Don't stop there—use pieces from incomplete board games, too, for a really unique frame!

Materials

Acrylic picture frame
Craft gems
Craft glue
Puzzle pieces

Instructions

1. Apply glue onto back of some puzzle pieces, then glue around edge of frame.

2. Repeat with remaining pieces for second layer.

3. Glue craft gems onto frame. Let dry.

IDEAS:

Checkers
Dominos
Dice
Scrabble® tiles
Mancala stones
Mini playing cards

CD Sunbonnet Earring Cushion

Materials

Craft glue

Craft scissors

Fabric: 45"-wide (⅓ yd)

Recycled CD

Ribbons: ½"-wide (⅓ yd); ¾"-wide (⅔ yd)

Serrated steak knife

Sharp craft scissors

Silk flower

Styrofoam™ ball: 3"

Instructions

1. Using craft scissors, cut 6½" circle from fabric. Cut 9" circle from fabric.

2. Using knife, cut Styrofoam™ ball in half.

3. Place 9" fabric circle, wrong side up, on flat surface. Center CD on fabric circle. Spread a thin line of glue around edge of fabric circle and around center hole of CD. Glue fabric to CD, moving from top to bottom then to the two sides. Evenly gather remaining fabric between these points. Using fingers, press fabric flat while gluing in place.

4. Place 6½" fabric, wrong side down, on flat surface. Spread a thin line of glue around outside edge of fabric circle. Center half-ball, flat side up onto fabric circle. Gather fabric evenly around ball, gluing fabric to flat side of ball.

5. Spread a generous amount of glue onto flat side of ball then glue to center of CD, covering glued fabric edges for hat. Hold firmly in place until glue begins to bond.

6. Glue ⅛"-wide ribbon around base of hat, forming hatband. Tie ¾"-wide ribbon in a bow and glue to hatband. Glue silk flower to center of bow.

85

Darling Diary

Everyone needs a special diary to record his or her most private thoughts. It is a snap to make from a notepad and scrapbook papers.

Instructions

1 Using glue stick, glue a piece of scrapbook paper to notepad front for background. Using decorative-edged scissors, cut and glue contrasting scrapbook papers as desired.

2 Measure notepad and add 3" to length. Using decorative-edged scissors, cut cardboard to those dimensions for cover.

3 Align cover with notepad bottom, extending cover 3" over the top.

4 Using craft knife and ruler, score cover, making it fold smoothly.

5 Using craft glue, glue cover onto back and over the top edge of notepad. Let dry.

6 Using craft scissors, cut small frame from cardboard. Cover with scrapbook paper. Using craft glue, glue craft gems and ribbon onto frame and notepad front as desired. Apply stickers as desired.

7 Using craft glue, glue frame to center front of notepad. Let dry.

Glue Hints:

What kind of glue do you use for what kinds of materials?

Use paste glue, like a glue stick, for gluing papers. Paste glue won't make your papers buckle.

Use craft glue to glue three-dimensional or heavier objects to surfaces. It is stronger and will get under the entire surface of an odd-shaped object and hold it in place.

Materials

Cardboard
Craft gems
Craft glue
Craft knife
Craft scissors
Decorative-edged scissors
Glue stick
Notepad
Ribbon scraps
Ruler
Scrapbook papers: assorted
Stickers (2)

MOSAIC BiRDHOUSE

Do you ever wish you could display all your little treasures gathered from fast-food restaurants, gumball machines, and loot bags? You can! Paint a birdhouse and adhere all these decorative items to the roof with plaster of paris.

Instructions

Note: Mosaic Birdhouse is for indoor use only.

1 Paint birdhouse with paints as desired. See photograph on facing page.

2 Mix plaster of paris, following manufacturer's instructions.

3 Spread some plaster onto roof and insert treasure. Continue until entire roof is covered. Let dry overnight.

Materials

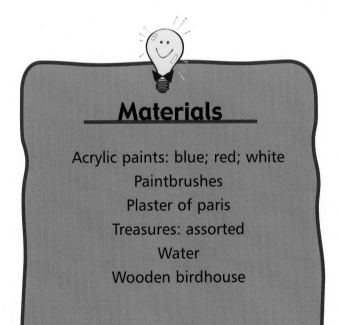

Acrylic paints: blue; red; white
Paintbrushes
Plaster of paris
Treasures: assorted
Water
Wooden birdhouse

IDEA:

This technique can be used on a picture frame or box top. To lower the cost of the project, glue treasures onto the top of a papier-mâché box.

Gifts

EDDIE'S BIRTHDAY MAY 18TH

SNOWMAN CARDS

One potato, two potato, three potato, four. Make potato-print cards, and they'll all want more. A half of a potato and a little paint are all you need to get started making these adorable holiday cards.

Instructions

1 Using decorative-edged scissors, cut 3¾" x 5" rectangle from patterned paper. Using decorative-edged scissors, cut 3" square from bright blue card stock. Glue patterned rectangle onto center front of card.

2 Using kitchen knife, cut potato in half. Blot cut ends of potato onto a paper towel until dry, creating stamp for snowman's head. *Note: One potato will make two stamps.*

3 Pour a quarter-sized amount of white paint onto paper plate.

Materials

Acrylic paint: white

Blank greeting card: white, standard size

Card stocks: black; bright blue; orange; yellow

Decorative-edged scissors: pinking

Glue pen

Hole punches: ¼"; ⁹⁄₁₆"

Household sponge: 2"-square

Kitchen knife

Paintbrush

Paper plate

Paper towels

Patterned paper: lt. blue

Potato

Star craft punch: ½"

4 Using one side of sponge, daub paint onto stamp, covering entire area.

5 Press stamp down firmly on center of bright blue square, then lift stamp straight up so that paint does not smear. Using paintbrush, touch up as necessary with white paint. Let dry.

6 Using ⁹⁄₁₆" hole punch, punch out one dot from orange card stock for nose. Using ¼" hole punch, punch out nine dots from black card stock for eyes and mouth. Using craft punch, punch six stars from yellow card stock.

7 Glue nose onto center of stamped head. See photograph on page 91. Center and glue eyes above nose. Evenly space and glue remaining circles under nose, creating a smiling face.

8 Glue square slightly off-center onto rectangle.

9 Randomly glue stars onto card front around snowman's head.

Christmas Card Ornaments

6 Using pinking scissors, cut out shape ¼" larger all around from felt.

7 Glue card cutout onto underside of glass puddle. Glue small felt cutout onto underside of card cutout.

8 Using craft scissors, cut 10" piece of cord. Fold cord in half then glue 2" of ends onto back of small felt cutout for hanger.

9 Glue large felt cutout onto back of small felt cutout, sandwiching hanger ends between felt layers. Let dry.

Materials

Clear glass puddles
Cord: metallic gold
Craft scissors
Decorative-edged scissors: pinking
Felt: assorted colors
Glass glue
Pencil
Recycled Christmas cards
Ruler

Instructions

1 Place puddle on top of desired area on Christmas card. Trace around puddle.

2 Using craft scissors, cut out shape from card.

3 Place puddle on top of coordinating color of felt. Trace around puddle.

4 Using pinking scissors, cut out shape ⅛" larger all around from felt.

5 Place puddle on top of a second color of felt. Trace around puddle.

Instructions

1 Using paper cutter, cut card stocks into various sizes. Fold in half for cards.

2 Trim decorative paper so that it is slightly smaller than card front. Glue decorative papers onto cards.

3 Using craft punches, punch out shapes from decorative papers. Glue onto cards.

4 Using hole punch, punch hole in top folded corner of card and thread with ribbon.

IDEAS:

Try combining the punchouts together to create something new. For example, string a few gingerbread punchouts together, side by side, for a paper chain or glue several hearts in a circle to create a flower.

Use the paper that has been punched as a stencil.

When using decorative punches, both the punchouts and the paper that has been punched are usable for card making.

Handmade cards are always appreciated and they are so much fun to make. Gather friends or family together and host a card-making party. Have everyone bring papers, ribbons, decorative craft punches, and craft glue. Sharing the supplies is half the fun. And, best of all, everyone will go home with beautiful handmade cards to send this holiday season.

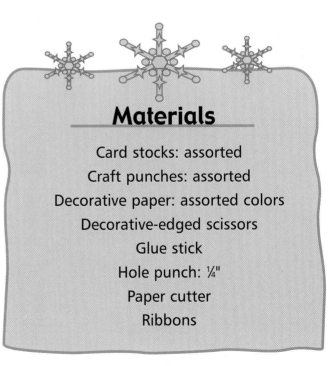

Materials

Card stocks: assorted

Craft punches: assorted

Decorative paper: assorted colors

Decorative-edged scissors

Glue stick

Hole punch: ¼"

Paper cutter

Ribbons

97

Snowman Door Hanger

Instructions

1 Place two craft sticks on wooden block. Drill a hole in two craft sticks as shown in Diagram A.

Diagram A

2 Paint one side of craft sticks with white paint. Let dry. Paint ¾" of drilled ends with black paint. Let dry. Repeat for remaining sides.

3 Paint one side of one mini craft stick with black paint for hat brim. Paint one mini craft stick with country blue paint for scarf. Paint circle and heart with country blue paint for scarf. Paint teardrop with orange paint for nose. Let dry. Repeat for remaining sides.

Materials

Acrylic paints: black; country blue; olive green; orange; red; white

Cord (10")

Craft glue

Craft sticks (5)

Extrafine-tipped pen: opaque white

Fine-tipped permanent marker with bullet: black

Mini craft sticks (2)

Paintbrushes

Paper towels

Power drill/drill bit: ³⁄₃₂"

Wooden block (scrap)

Wooden circle: ⅜"

Wooden heart: 1"

Wooden teardrop: ⅞"

4 Glue craft sticks side by side for snowman body. See photograph on facing page. Center and glue hat brim onto snowman body.

Continued on page 100.

Continued from page 99.

5 Using bullet end of marker, dot eyes below hat brim. Using fine-tipped end, draw mouth below eyes. Outline nose and scarf pieces.

6 Using opaque pen, outline hat and hat brim.

7 See Dry-brushing on page 13. Dry-brush cheek area with red paint.

8 Using end of paintbrush handle, dot cheek area with white paint for cheeks.

9 Using end of paintbrush handle, dot an evenly spaced row inside scarf outline pieces with olive green paint. Let dry.

10 Glue nose below eyes, overlapping mouth. Let dry.

11 Glue tip of heart onto one end of hat brim. Glue circle onto tip of heart. See photograph on page 98. Glue scarf below nose. Let dry.

12 Using bullet end of marker, dot buttons down front of snowman.

13 Dot glue onto ends of cord and twist each end into a point.

14 Insert cord ends into holes in hat, going from front to back. Knot cord ends for hanger.

IDEAS:

Use the Snowman Door Hanger as a tree ornament.

Make a doorknob hanger for each season. Vary the colors of the hat and a scarf to match the season. Try the following instead of drawing on the black buttons:

For spring: Paint Easter eggs on for buttons.

For summer: Paint beach balls on for buttons.

For fall: Paint leaves or pumpkins on for buttons.

CRAB BASKET

CRAB BASKET

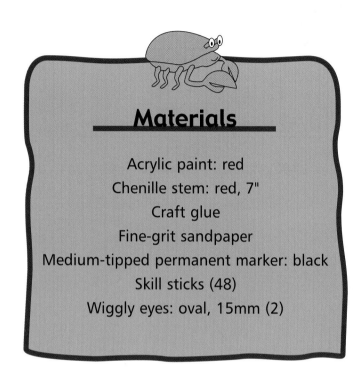

Materials

Acrylic paint: red
Chenille stem: red, 7"
Craft glue
Fine-grit sandpaper
Medium-tipped permanent marker: black
Skill sticks (48)
Wiggly eyes: oval, 15mm (2)

Instructions

1 Lightly sand all skill sticks.

2 Line up twelve skill sticks vertically side by side, for a 4½"-square base. Evenly space and glue five skill sticks horizontally across base as shown in Diagram A.

Diagram A

3 Connect and glue together four skill sticks for body sides as shown in Diagram B. Continue building up with skill sticks until sides are five sticks high. Run a bead of glue along the inside corner of each side.

Diagram B

4 Set aside two skill sticks.

5 Snap off and discard a single section from one end of eight skill sticks for legs.

6 Snap off and set aside double section from each end of one skill stick. Discard remaining pieces of stick.

7 Glue one double section onto one whole skill stick for front claw. See photograph on page 101. Repeat for remaining double section and whole skill stick for arms.

8 Paint one side of arms, legs, base, and sides with red paint. Let dry. Repeat for remaining sides.

9 Turn base over so that horizontal sticks are on top. Glue arms and legs onto top of horizontal sticks, with snapped ends touching, and position as shown in Diagram C. Let dry.

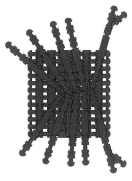

Diagram C

10 Turn base over and glue body sides squarely onto top of base for basket.

11 Fold chenille stem in half. Glue one eye onto each end of stem. Let dry. Bend stem ends forward. Glue fold of stem onto base at inside center front of basket. Let dry.

12 Draw mouth in center of second skill stick from bottom on front of crab.

Spring Plant Stakes

Materials

Acrylic paints: lavender; med. pink; tangerine; lt. yellow

Craft glue

Craft scissors

Feathers: yellow, 2"-long (2)

Fine-tipped permanent marker with bullet: black

Jumbo craft stick

Paintbrush: #6, round

Satin ribbon: blue, ¼"-wide (¼ yd)

Wooden circle: 1¼"-diameter

Wooden octagon: 1½"

Wooden triangle: 1"

Instructions
(for Chick Plant Stake)

1 Paint one side of craft stick with lavender paint for stake. Paint circle for head and octagon for body with lt. yellow paint. Paint triangle with tangerine paint for beak. Let dry. Repeat for remaining sides.

2 Using bullet end of marker, draw eyes on head. Using fine-tipped end, draw nostrils on beak.

3 Using end of paintbrush handle, dot cheeks on head with med. pink paint.

4 Glue feathers symmetrically onto back of body for wings. Glue head onto center top of body as shown in Diagram A. Glue beak onto head. Glue stake vertically onto bottom back of body.

Diagram A

5 Using end of paintbrush handle, dot an evenly spaced row down center of stake with med. pink paint. Let dry.

6 Tie ribbon into a bow. Trim bow ends diagonally. Center and glue bow under head. Let dry.

105

Instructions
(for Egg Plant Stake)

1 Paint one side of craft stick with olive green paint for stake. Paint egg with lt. blue paint. Paint small circle with lt. yellow paint for flower center. Let dry. Repeat for remaining sides.

2 Center and glue flower center onto egg.

3 Using end of paintbrush handle, dot an evenly spaced row around flower center with white paint for flower petals. See photograph below. Let dry.

Materials

Acrylic paints: lt. blue; olive green; dk. pink; white; lt. yellow
Craft glue
Jumbo craft stick
Paintbrush: #6, round
Wooden circle: ⅜"-diameter
Wooden egg: 1½"
Wooden octagon: 1½"

4 Glue stake vertically onto bottom back of egg.

5 Using end of paintbrush handle, dot an evenly spaced row down center of stake with dk. pink paint. Let dry.

4 Glue ears onto back of head. Glue nose onto front of head. Glue head onto center top of body.

5 Glue pom-pom onto left side of body. See photograph at left.

6 Glue stake vertically onto bottom back of body.

7 Using end of paintbrush handle, dot an evenly spaced row down center of craft stick with dk. pink paint. Let dry.

8 Tie ribbon into a bow. Evenly trim bow ends. Center and glue bow under head. Let dry.

Instructions
(for Bunny Plant Stake)

1 Paint one side of craft stick with tangerine paint for stake. Paint octagon for body, teardrops for ears, and large circle for head with white paint. Paint small circle with lt. pink paint for nose. Let dry. Repeat for remaining sides.

2 Using end of paintbrush handle, dot cheeks on head with dk. pink paint.

3 Using bullet end of marker, draw eyes on head. Using fine-tipped end, draw a line vertically from center of head as shown in Diagram A.

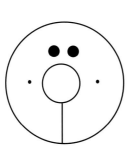

Diagram A

Materials

Acrylic paints: dk. pink; lt. pink; tangerine; white
Craft glue
Craft scissors
Fine-tipped permanent maker with bullet
Jumbo craft stick
Paintbrush: #6, round
Pom-pom: metallic white, ⅜"
Satin ribbon: ¼"-wide (¼ yd)
Wooden circles: ⅜"-diameter; 1¼"-diameter
Wooden octagon: 1½"
Wooden teardrops: 1½" (2)

107

Treasure Containers

These decorative glass containers will make a beautiful gift anyone would love to receive.

Instructions

1 Paint glass container with nail polish as desired. Let dry.

Note: If you make a mistake, remove polish with nail polish remover.

2 Tie ribbon scraps around containers as desired.

IDEA:

Treasure Containers can be filled with fresh or silk flowers, candy, special keepsakes, or a candle.

Note: Keep ribbons and/or other flammables away from candle flame.

Materials

Glass containers
Nail polish: assorted colors
Nail polish remover (optional)
Ribbons (scraps)

Cool Clothes

SOCCER
ESTD 1948

RETURN CHRIS'S SHIRT

Baseball Practice
at
9:00 am

Meeting at
7:00

Treasured Art Apron

Instructions

1 Photocopy desired artwork onto iron-on transfer paper.

2 Place transfer on apron as desired. Iron on artwork, following manufacturer's instructions.

Note: Iron-on transfer paper is available at most craft stores. However, some copy centers prefer using their own.

IDEAS:

Use fabric paint or fabric markers to add color or design to artwork.

Glue ribbons, buttons, or rhinestones around artwork, creating a frame.

To bring the cost down, transfer artwork onto an old T-shirt, pillowcase, or linen towel.

Materials

Apron
Child's artwork
Iron/ironing board
Iron-on transfer paper
Photocopier

Flower Power T-Shirt

Instructions

1 Scrunch up T-shirt and wrap rubber bands unevenly, beginning at the bottom of sleeves and working up to neckline, then down to hem. Overlap rubber bands as you work.

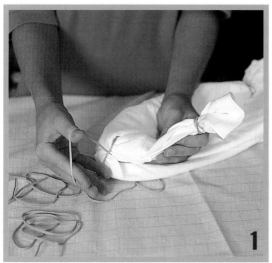

Materials

Acrylic paints: fuchsia; lavender; orange; pink; primary yellow

Cardboard

Child's T-shirt: white

Clothes dryer

Cold water

Daisy rubber stamps: one for each paint color (5)

Fabric dye: teal

Fabric medium

Paper plate (2)

Rubber bands

Saucepan: large

Sponge brush

2 Mix dye in saucepan and dye T-shirt, following manufacturer's instructions. Rinse shirt with cold water. Remove rubber bands. Dry T-shirt in dryer, then press.

3 Lay T-shirt out flat on work surface. Place cardboard inside T-shirt between front and back. *Note: This will keep paint from going through to other side.*

4 Pour a quarter-sized amount of each paint color onto paper plates. *Note: Use two plates if necessary.* Mix paints with fabric medium, following manufacturer's instructions. *Note: Fabric paint may also be used.*

5 Using sponge brush, daub paint onto stamp, covering entire area.

6 Randomly press stamp down firmly along top edge of dyed area on shirt front and sleeves, then lift stamp straight up so that paint does not smear. Repeat for remaining paint colors and stamps. See photograph on facing page. Let dry.

Jazzy Jeans

Materials

Buttons: assorted
Denim shorts or pants
Fabric glue
Ribbon (scraps)

Instructions

1 Position and generously glue ribbons onto jeans as desired. Fold over ribbon ends and overlap on inside of jean leg on seam.

2 Position and glue buttons onto ribbons and jeans as desired. Let dry overnight.

Note: Wash on gentle cycle in washing machine or wash by hand.

IDEAS:

Try creating patterns with buttons or layering buttons over ribbons.

Combining ribbons can create a whole new look, as well.

Sometimes we need to add a little zing to our wardrobe. Jazzing up your jeans is simple, and best of all, you are the fashion designer. Gather buttons and ribbon and start creating.

Fancy Footwear

Materials

Clear cement glue

Decorative elements: beaded
strands; rhinestones;
silk flowers

Nylon thread

Thongs

Instructions

1 Glue decorative elements onto
thongs.

2 Attach beaded strands to thongs
straps with thread. Knot to secure.

*Why settle for boring when you
can create beautiful? These
fancy thongs will be such fun
to wear.*

IDEAS:

Garden clogs can also be embellished.
Try embellishing canvas sneakers or
old house slippers.

SCRIMSHAW NECKLACE

Instructions

1 Mix plaster of paris and ⅔ cup of water until it reaches the consistency of runny mashed potatoes.

2 Place a spoonful of mixture onto waxed paper and flatten like a small pancake for medallion. Let dry.

3 Using craft knife, carefully carve two ⅛" holes at top of medallion. If desired, sand smooth.

4 Using craft knife, etch animals, scenery, or desired designs into medallion. *Note: The deeper the etches, the better the medallion will look.*

5 Using dry paintbrush, brush away dust from designs.

6 Using rag, rub over medallion with a dime-sized amount of paint. Let dry.

7 Thread cord through holes and knot cord ends for necklace.

In the mid 1800s, American whalers carved beautiful jewelry and decorative objects from whale tusks and called it scrimshaw. You can carve your own scrimshaw from plaster of paris.

Materials

Acrylic paints: assorted colors
Cord: ⅛"-wide (24")
Craft knife
Fine-grit sandpaper (optional)
Measuring cups
Metal spoon
Paintbrush
Plaster of paris
Soft rag
Water
Waxed paper

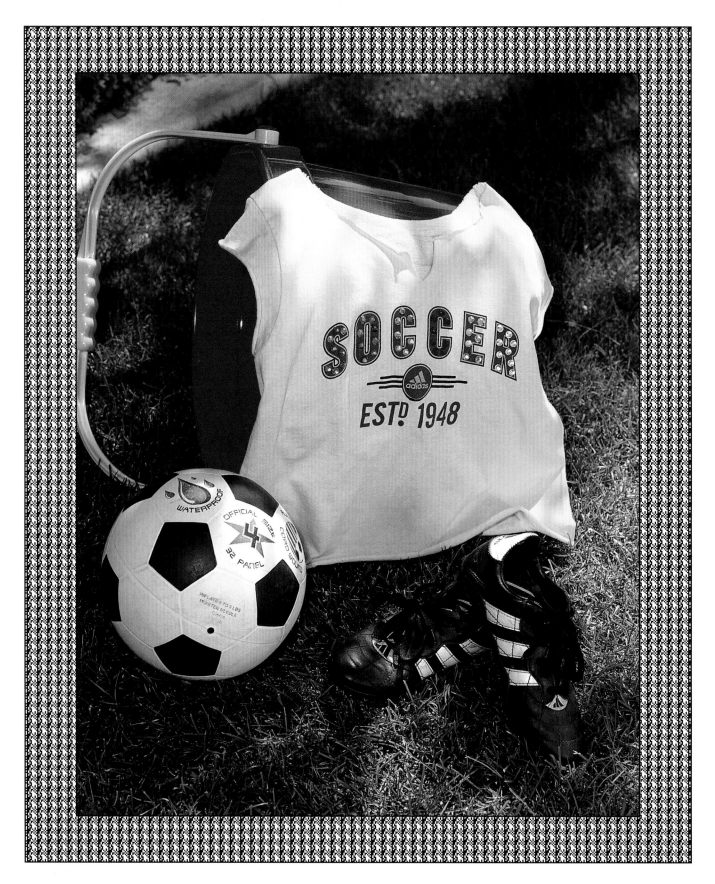

Soccer Shirt

Here's an idea taken right from the trendiest shops in New York City. . . . Take your old team shirt and give it a radical makeover, turning it into a completely cool new wardrobe standout.

Materials

Craft jewels: assorted colors
Craft scissors
Fabric dye (optional)
Fabric glue
Sports team shirt
Studs

Instructions

Note: If desired, dye shirt, following manufacturer's directions. Dry completely.

1 Cut off sleeves, neck ribbing and lower portion of shirt. *Note: The edges will curl a bit, but that is part of the look you are trying to achieve.*

2 Glue studs and jewels onto shirt to embellish the team writing.

IDEAS:

Try cutting a small "V" into the neckline for added interest

Instead of cutting off the entire sleeve, try leaving a bit of it, creating a cap sleeve.

Instead of cutting off the bottom of the shirt, cut the lower portion of the shirt in half vertically, creating two pieces you can tie together at your midriff.

Glue studs or jewels along neckline and sleeve line as embellishments.

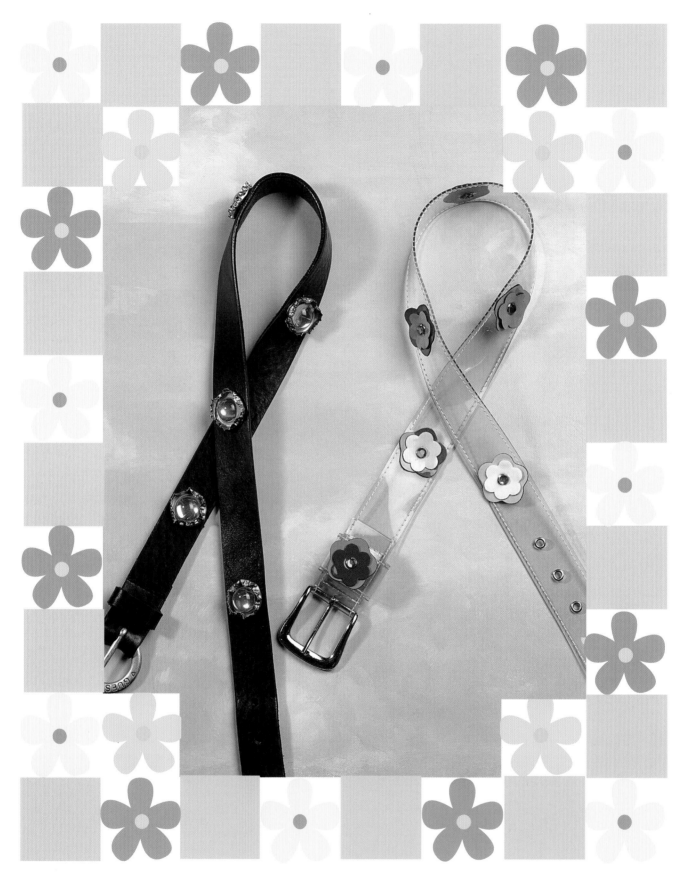

Fashion Belts

Instructions

(for Bottle Cap Belt)

Note: Make certain that bottle caps are clean and dry.

1 Hammer down any sharp edges on bottle caps.

2 Evenly space and glue bottle caps onto belt.

3 Center and glue flat-backed marbles into center of bottle caps. Let dry.

Materials

Belt: black

Clear cement glue

Flat-backed marbles: clear

Hammer

Old bottle caps (5)

Materials

Clear cement glue

Clear plastic belt with flowers

Rhinestones: 7mm (5)

Instructions

(for Flower Belt)

1 Glue rhinestones onto flower centers on belt. Let dry.

Mary Ayres began her designing career at around the age of three and has been designing ever since. She is a full-time designer, working on a variety of projects including kids' crafts, paper crafts, sew-ing, quilting, embroidery, and painting projects. She resides in Virginia with her husband Jerry. Mary's projects are featured on pages: 42–43, 58–63, 74–75, 78–81, 91–95, and 98–107.

Jill Grover works as an interior designer, decor-ating all over the world, and is the author of *Scary Scenes for Halloween, Handmade Giftwrap, Bows, Cards & Tags*, and *Dime Store Decorating: Flea Market Finds with Style*. She resides in Northern Utah with her husband and their three children— Laci, Levi, and River. Jill's projects are featured on pages: 28–29, 32–35, 48–49, 76–77, 118–119, and 124–125.

Kathleen George has been free-lance crafting and teaching art to all ages for almost 30 years in her home studio in Western Massachusetts. Her work has included product development, craft demonstrations, artist-in-residence projects in the public schools, and on-going after-school clay classes for ele-mentary children. Kathleen's projects are featured on pages: 40–41, 44–47, 50–51, 54–57, and 71–73.

Shauna Mooney Kawaski's pro-fessional career began in advertising, but was short-lived when her artistic talents were discovered by others. She was asked to be an art director for a national children's magazine and she enjoyed this position for 18 years. She has been involved in the writing, illustrating, and designing of over 20 books. Shauna's projects are featured on pages: 16–25, 36–37, 52–53, and 120–121.

Sheryl Quinn's project is featured on pages 84–85. She has loved doing crafts for as long as she can remember. Sheryl enjoys making crafts out of re-cycled items, and creating her own designs. She resides in Brunswick, Maine, with her husband, their two children, and two cats.

Metric Equivalency Chart

mm-millimetres cm-centimetres
inches to millimetres and centimetres

inches	mm	cm	inches	cm	inches	cm
⅛	3	0.3	9	22.9	30	76.2
¼	6	0.6	10	25.4	31	78.7
⅜	10	1.0	11	27.9	32	81.3
½	13	1.3	12	30.5	33	83.8
⅝	16	1.6	13	33.0	34	86.4
¾	19	1.9	14	35.6	35	88.9
⅞	22	2.2	15	38.1	36	91.4
1	25	2.5	16	40.6	37	94.0
1¼	32	3.2	17	43.2	38	96.5
1½	38	3.8	18	45.7	39	99.1
1¾	44	4.4	19	48.3	40	101.6
2	51	5.1	20	50.8	41	104.1
2½	64	6.4	21	53.3	42	106.7
3	76	7.6	22	55.9	43	109.2
3½	89	8.9	23	58.4	44	111.8
4	102	10.2	24	61.0	45	114.3
4½	114	11.4	25	63.5	46	116.8
5	127	12.7	26	66.0	47	119.4
6	152	15.2	27	68.6	48	121.9
7	178	17.8	28	71.1	49	124.5
8	203	20.3	29	73.7	50	127.0

yards to metres

yards	metres	yards	metres	yards	metres	yards	metres	yards	metres
⅛	0.11	2⅛	1.94	4⅛	3.77	6⅛	5.60	8⅛	7.43
¼	0.23	2¼	2.06	4¼	3.89	6¼	5.72	8¼	7.54
⅜	0.34	2⅜	2.17	4⅜	4.00	6⅜	5.83	8⅜	7.66
½	0.46	2½	2.29	4½	4.11	6½	5.94	8½	7.77
⅝	0.57	2⅝	2.40	4⅝	4.23	6⅝	6.06	8⅝	7.89
¾	0.69	2¾	2.51	4¾	4.34	6¾	6.17	8¾	8.00
⅞	0.80	2⅞	2.63	4⅞	4.46	6⅞	6.29	8⅞	8.12
1	0.91	3	2.74	5	4.57	7	6.40	9	8.23
1⅛	1.03	3⅛	2.86	5⅛	4.69	7⅛	6.52	9⅛	8.34
1¼	1.14	3¼	2.97	5¼	4.80	7¼	6.63	9¼	8.46
1⅜	1.26	3⅜	3.09	5⅜	4.91	7⅜	6.74	9⅜	8.57
1½	1.37	3½	3.20	5½	5.03	7½	6.86	9½	8.69
1⅝	1.49	3⅝	3.31	5⅝	5.14	7⅝	6.97	9⅝	8.80
1¾	1.60	3¾	3.43	5¾	5.26	7¾	7.09	9¾	8.92
1⅞	1.71	3⅞	3.54	5⅞	5.37	7⅞	7.20	9⅞	9.03

Index